SuperTots 3

Student Book

Chip

Peter

Beth

Grandma

Sammy

Toni

JESSIE

Aleda Krause   Michelle Nagashima

bed

bookcase

table

chair

sofa

Do it!

1 Wipe the table.

2 Wash the dishes.

3 Put away the dishes.

4 Make the bed.

Use it!

Wipe the table, please.

OK.

actions and dialog

4

an apartment

Olia

a tent

Erdene

a wooden house

Ngawaiata

a bamboo house

Edgar

Bb

Gg

Mm

Pp

Ss

Tt

park

library

zoo

museum

beach

farm

1

2

3

4

5

6

7

8

1 Turn on the computer.

2 Put in the disk.

3 Click the mouse.

4 Take out the disk.

Use it!

Did you turn on the computer?

Yes, I did.

actions and dialog

14

Cc

Dd

Ff

Hh

Jj

Rr

Unit 3
Community Helpers

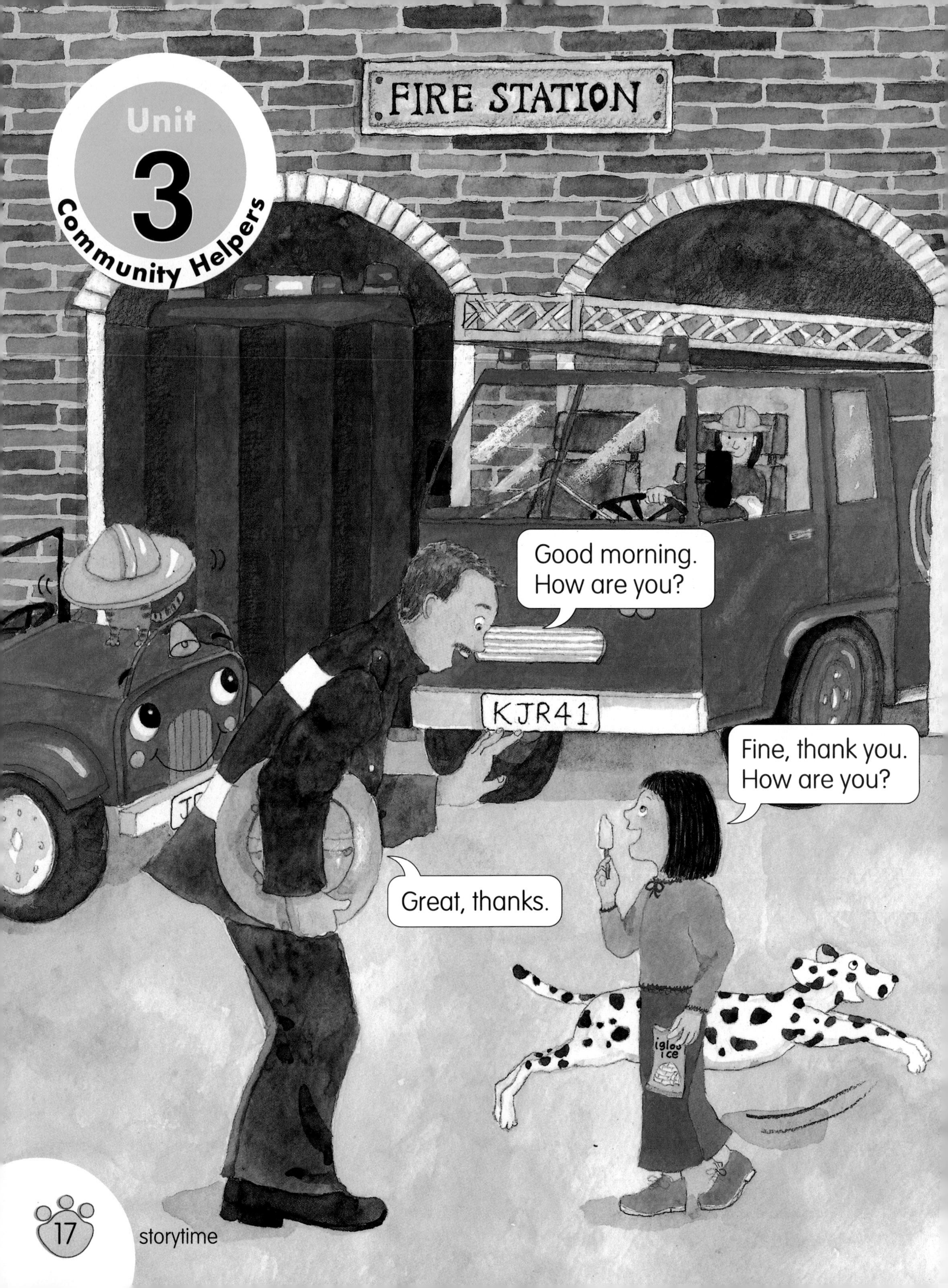

S 75

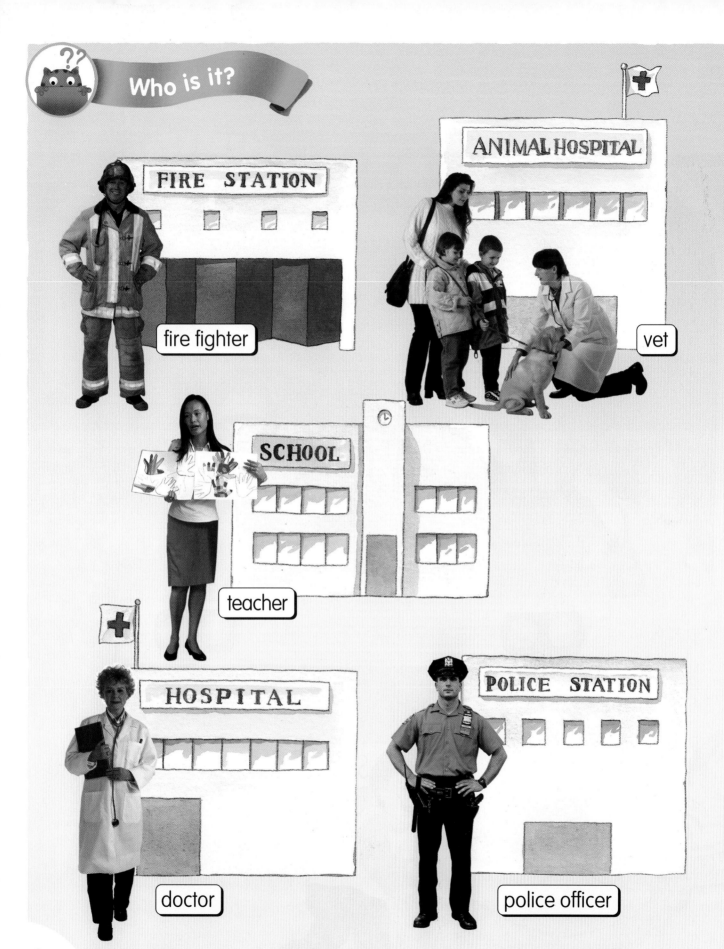

fire fighter

vet

teacher

doctor

police officer

1 Turn the wheel.

2 Pull the hose.

3 Push the button.

4 Ring the bell.

Use it!

Can you turn the wheel?

Yes, I can.

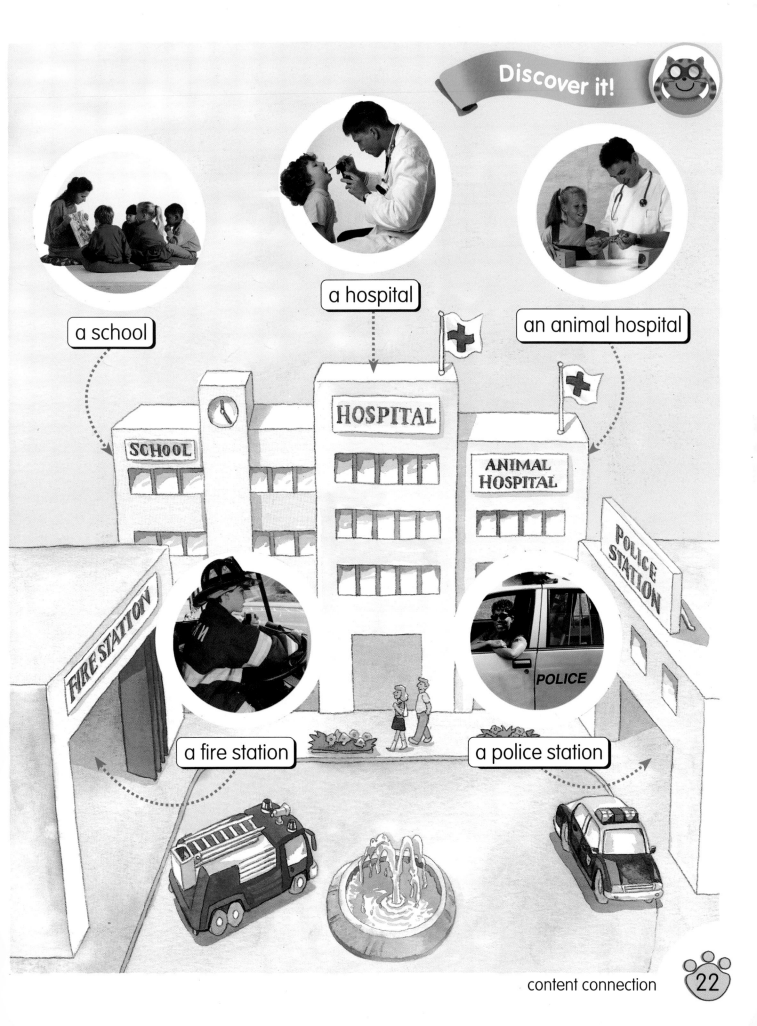

a school

a hospital

an animal hospital

a fire station

a police station

I i

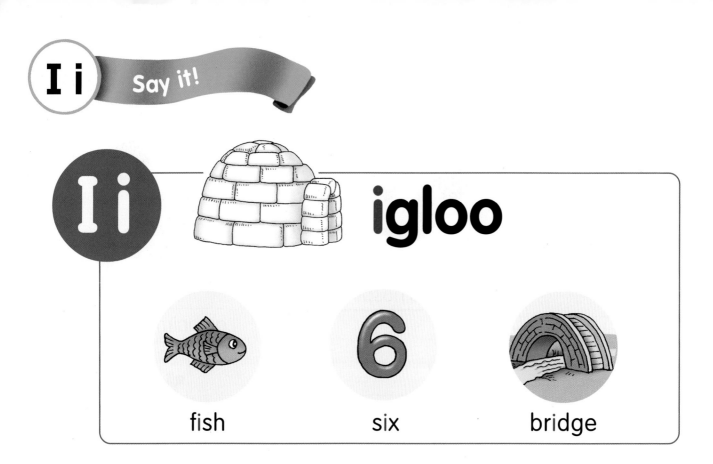

I i

igloo

fish

six

bridge

sounds

A B C D E F G H **I** J K L M N O P Q R S T U V W X Y Z

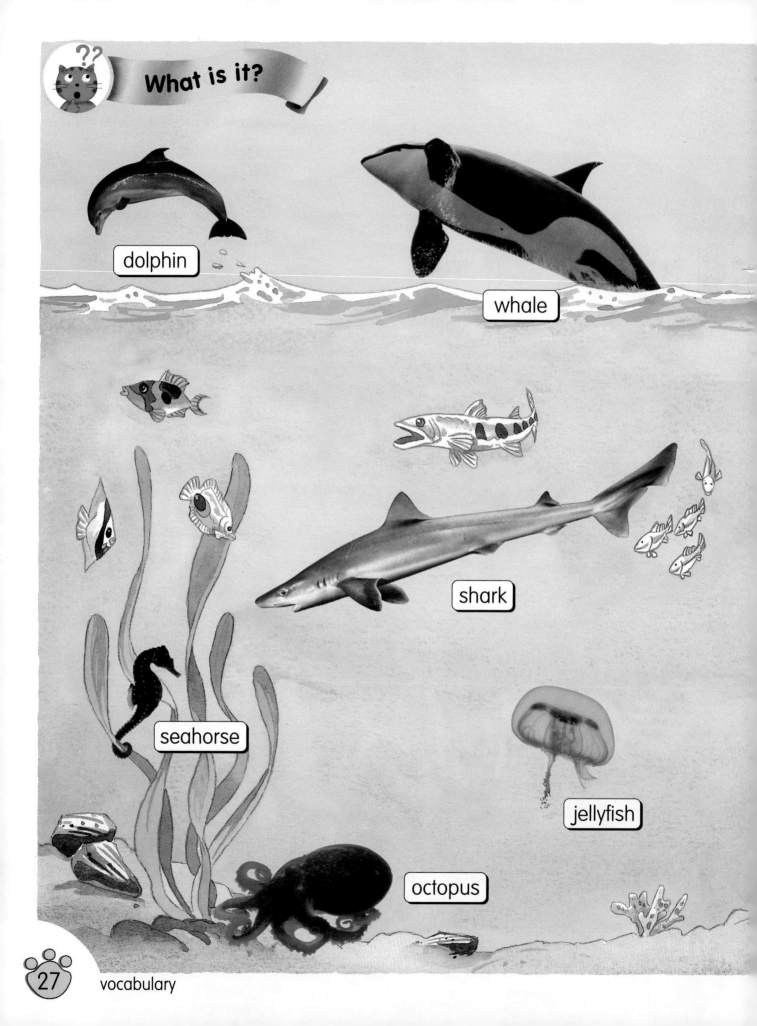

dolphin

whale

shark

seahorse

jellyfish

octopus

vocabulary

Do it!

1 Pick up the newspaper.

2 Throw away the bottle.

3 Fold the plastic bag.

4 Crush the can.

Use it!

Let's pick up the newspaper.

OK.

actions and dialog

Put litter in the trashcan.

Recycle.

Plant a tree.

Save water.

Oo Say it!

octopus

rock

hop

socks

lion

gorilla

elephant

bat

fox

zebra

1 Fly.

2 Climb.

3 Jump.

4 Swim.

Can a lion fly?

No! Can an elephant jump?

No!

actions and dialog

food

water

a clean home

love

Ee   Say it!

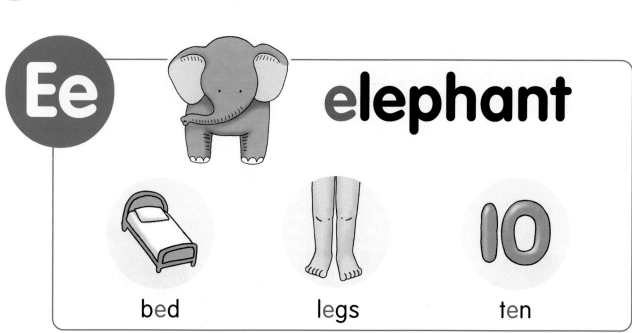

Ee   e**lephant**

bed   legs   ten

Weather Around the World

What's it like?

raining

sunny

snowing

hot

cold

1 Get in line.

2 Buy a ticket.

3 Go inside.

4 Be quiet.

Use it!

Get in line, please.

OK.

planets

stars

the moon

the sun

a shooting star

Uu   Say it!

umbrella

bus

jump

run

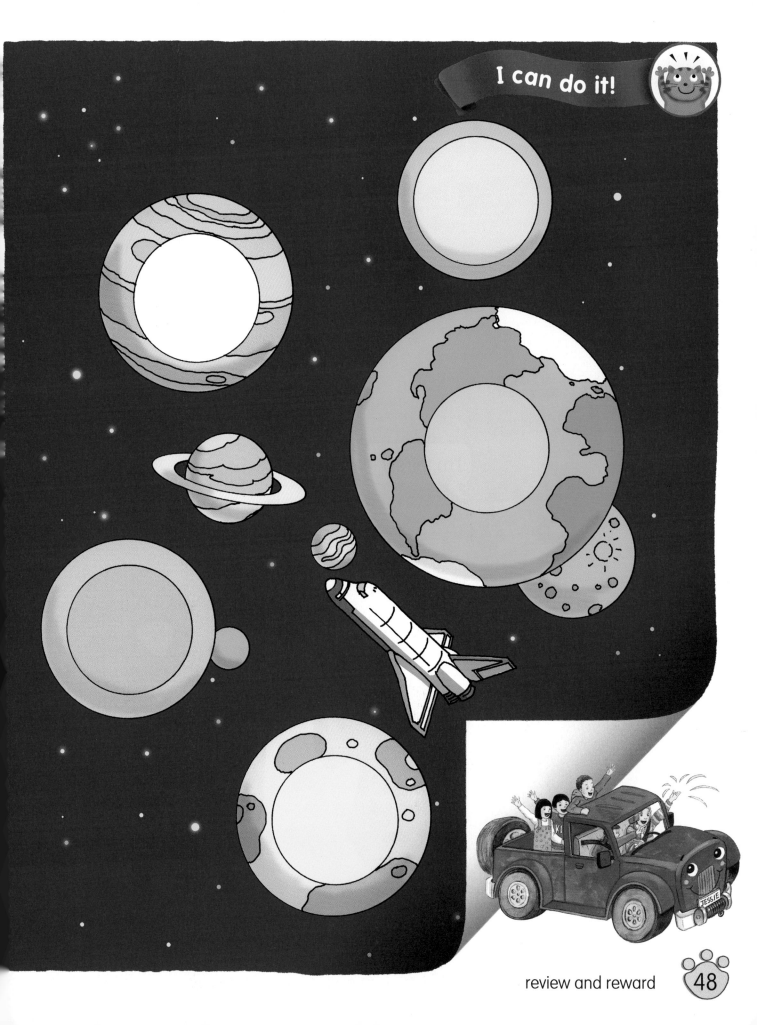

TESSIE

plant

yogurt

cow

chicken

egg

cheese

Do it!

1 Make a hole.

2 Put in the seed.

3 Cover up the seed.

4 Give it water.

Use it!

Did you give it water?

Oops. No, I didn't.

actions and dialog 52

seeds

water

fruit

tomato

flowers

sun

Aa

Aa **apple**

cat

bat

tag

slippery seaweed

rough starfish

smooth shell

1 Put on sunscreen.

2 Run to the water.

3 Splash in the waves.

4 Dry off.

Let's put on sunscreen.

OK.

a crab

a rock

a starfish

a shell

seaweed

content connection

Kk

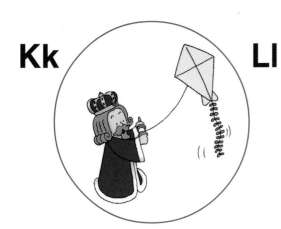

Ll

Nn

Qq

Vv

Ww

Xx

Yy

Zz

JESSIE

Crafts

Grandma's House

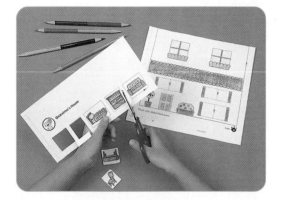

1. Color and cut out the house and furniture.

2. Fold the house in half and glue the furniture into the rooms.

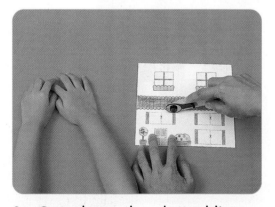

3. Cut along the dotted lines on the door and windows.*

4. Fold the doors and windows open.

* Ask an adult to help.

Day Trip Mini Book

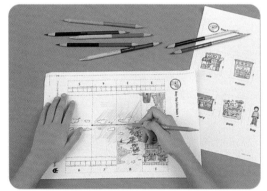

1. Color and cut out the template, places, and boy or girl.

2. Fold the template to make a mini book.

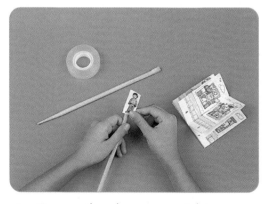

3. Glue the places into the pages of the mini book.

4. Tape the boy or girl to a chopstick.

Community Helpers Flip Book

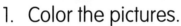

1. Color the pictures.

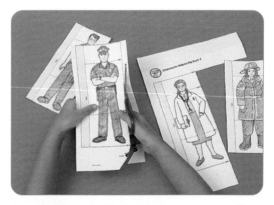

2. Cut out the pictures on the solid lines.

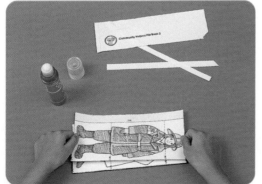

3. Glue the 4 pictures together to make a book.

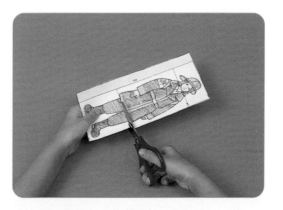

4. Cut the book on the dotted lines.

Octopus Craft

1. Use newspaper to make the octopus body.

2. Cover it with crepe paper and tape it at the base.

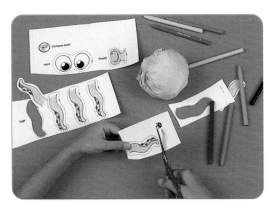

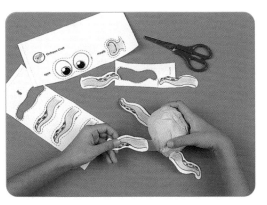

3. Color and cut out the octopus eyes, mouth, and legs.

4. Tape them to the octopus body.

Animal Masks

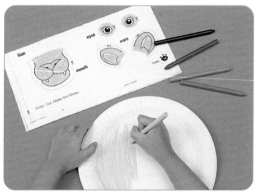
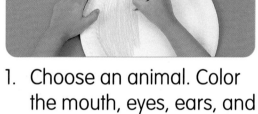

1. Choose an animal. Color the mouth, eyes, ears, and paper plate.

2. Cut out the eyes, ears, and mouth and glue them to the plate.

3. Decorate the mask with colored paper.

4. Staple a strip of card to each side of the mask.*

* Ask an adult to help.

Space Travel Craft

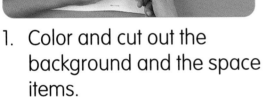

1. Color and cut out the background and the space items.

2. Attach the planet and glue the background to some card.

3. Cut a slit along the dotted line.*

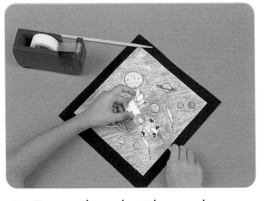

4. Tape the shuttle and astronaut to a chopstick.

* Ask an adult to help.

Plant Life Craft

1. Color and cut out the movie strips and flower.

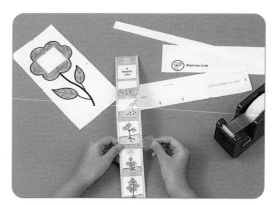

2. Tape the movie strips together.

3. Cut along the dotted lines in the flower.

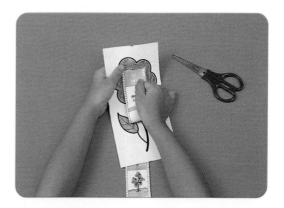

4. Feed the movie strip through the flower.

Tide Pool Craft

1. Color the inside base of a paper plate and the tide pool items.

2. Cut out and glue the tide pool items to the paper plate.

3. Cut out the base of a second paper plate.

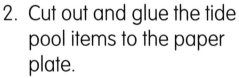

4. Color the rim and tape the plates together.

Picture Dictionary

1 one   **2** two   **3** three   **4** four   **5** five   **6** six   **7** seven   **8** eight   **9** nine   **10** ten

red   blue   yellow   green   orange   brown   black   white   pink   purple

apple	cheese	egg	
bat 	chicken	elephant	
beach 	Chip	farm	
bed 	cold	fire fighter	
Beth	cow	fox	
bookcase	doctor	gorilla	
chair	dolphin	Grandma	

hot	raining	sunny 
igloo	rough	table
jellyfish	Sammy	teacher
Jessie	seahorse	Toni
library	seaweed	umbrella
lion	shark 	vet
museum	shell	whale
octopus	slippery 	yogurt
park 	smooth	zebra
Peter	snowing 	zoo
plant 	sofa	
police officer	starfish	

Alphabet Chart

Aa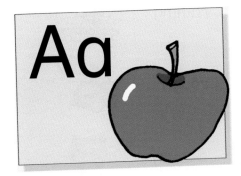

Bb

Ff

Gg

Hh

Ll

Mm

Nn

Rr

Ss

Tt

Xx

Yy

Zz

Cc

Dd

Ee

Ii
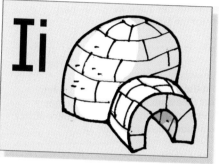

Jj

Kk

Oo

Pp

Qq

Uu

Vv

Ww

apple • bookcase • cow • dolphin • elephant • fire fighter • gorilla • house

igloo • jellyfish • king • lion • moon • newspaper • octopus • plant • queen

rabbit • sofa • table • umbrella • vet • whale • fox • yogurt • zebra

Syllabus

Unit	Topics/Goals	Talk about it!/Storyline	What is it?
Unit 1	Ask about and introduce someone Request help politely Offer and accept help Name furniture Do helping at home actions Learn about homes around the world	**Helping Grandma** Peter and Toni arrive at Grandma's house with their friends, Beth and Chip. Grandma is in the yard doing some gardening. Toni introduces her friends. The children help Grandma with the chores. They learn about other children's homes around the world. Then they leave for their first adventure in Grandma's magical car, Jessie the Jeep.	table chair sofa bookcase bed
Unit 2	Ask and say where you are going Invite friends to come over Ask about past actions Name places to visit Do using a computer actions Learn about fairytale characters	**The Library** Grandma takes the children to the library. They look at places they would like to visit, some in books, others on the computer. Then they go to the reading corner and Grandma reads them a fairytale. Grandma's magic brings the characters out of the book. Grandma uses her magic to change Jessie into a fire truck ready for the next adventure.	library zoo beach farm museum park
Unit 3	Review greetings Ask about ability Say what you want to be Name community helpers Do using equipment actions Learn about where community helpers work	**Community Helpers** Grandma and the children visit a fire station, where they get to climb on the fire truck and try out the equipment. The children play at dress up and say what they want to be when they grow up. They learn about where community helpers work. Grandma changes Jessie into a submarine ready for the next adventure.	fire fighter vet teacher doctor police officer
Unit 4	Ask and say whose turn it is Ask and say how many things you see Make a suggestion Name sea creatures Review numbers 1-10 Do recycling actions Learn ways to help the environment	**An Undersea Adventure** Grandma takes the children under the sea on an adventure. They take turns driving the submarine and counting the fish. They learn about ways to help the environment. Grandma changes Jessie into a hot air balloon ready for the next adventure.	octopus dolphin shark seahorse jellyfish whale numbers 1-10
Unit 5	Ask and say where something is Ask about animals' abilities Ask and say what you are Name wild animals Do animal movement actions Learn how to care for pets	**A Night Safari** Grandma takes the children on a night safari. They see many different animals. Then they have fun trying on animal masks. They learn how to care for pets. Grandma changes Jessie into a space shuttle ready for the next adventure.	elephant bat gorilla lion zebra fox
Unit 6	Ask and talk about the weather Make a polite command Say what you want to see Name kinds of weather Do seeing an exhibit actions Learn about things in the sky	**The Science Museum** Grandma and the children go to the science museum where they learn about the weather all over the world. They buy tickets to see the space shuttle. Then they learn about things in the sky. Grandma changes Jessie into a pick-up truck ready for the next adventure.	raining sunny snowing hot cold
Unit 7	Say you are thirsty and offer a drink Ask about past actions Ask who's hungry Name farm animals and products Do planting a seed actions Learn about the life cycle of a plant	**A Farm Visit** Grandma takes the children to a farm where they look at the farm animals, eat and drink farm products, and learn about the life cycle of a plant. Grandma changes Jessie into a speed boat ready for the final adventure.	cow yogurt cheese chicken egg plant
Unit 8	Show something you find and describe it Make a suggestion Thank someone for a good time Say how something feels Do going for a swim actions Learn about things in a tide pool	**The Beach** Grandma takes the children to the beach. They explore a tide pool and talk about how things feel. Then they go swimming. All their families join them and they have a party on the beach. Beth thanks Grandma for so many wonderful adventures.	slippery seaweed rough starfish smooth shell

Crafts Grandma's House, Day Trip Mini Book, Community Helpers Flip Book, Octopus Craft, Animal Masks, Space Travel Craft, Plant Life Craft, Tide Pool Craft

Dialogs	Do it!	Sing it!/Chant it!	Say it!	Discover it!
1) Hello. Who's this? My friend, Chip. Nice to meet you. Nice to meet you. 2) Wipe the table, please./OK. 3) Can I help? Yes, please.	Wipe the table. Wash the dishes. Put away the dishes. Make the bed.	1) Hello. Who's this? Song 2) Helping Chant 3) Can I help? Song 4) Sounds Rap 1	Review of: **Bb** **Gg** **Mm** **Pp** **Ss** **Tt**	**Homes around the world** an apartment a tent a wooden house a bamboo house
1) Where are we going? To the library. 2) Hey, everybody. Over here! OK. 3) Did you turn on the computer? Yes, I did.	Turn on the computer. Put in the disk. Click the mouse. Take out the disk.	1) Where are we going? Song 2) Hey, everybody! Song 3) Computer Chant 4) Sounds Rap 2	Review of: **Cc** **Dd** **Ff** **Hh** **Jj** **Rr**	**Fairytale** king queen princess wizard dragon castle crown
1) Good morning. How are you?/Fine, thank you. How are you?/Great, thanks. 2) Can you turn the wheel? Yes, I can. 3) I want to be a fire fighter. Not me. I want to be a vet.	Turn the wheel. Pull the hose. Push the button. Ring the bell.	1) Good morning. Song 2) Turn the wheel. Chant 3) I want to be a fire fighter. Song 4) Igloo Rap	**Ii** igloo fish six bridge	**At work** a fire station an animal hospital a school a hospital a police station
1) Whose turn is it? Yours. 2) How many jellyfish can you see? One, two, three, four, five! 3) Let's pick up the newspaper. OK.	Pick up the newspaper. Throw away the bottle. Fold the plastic bag. Crush the can.	1) Whose turn is it? Chant 2) How many jellyfish? Song 3) Recycle Chant 4) Octopus Rap	**Oo** octopus rock hop socks	**Help our world** Put litter in the trashcan. Recycle. Plant a tree. Save water.
1) Where's the elephant? Over there, in the water. 2) Can a lion fly?/No! Can an elephant jump?/No! 3) What are you? I'm a lion!/Cool!	Fly. Climb. Jump. Swim.	1) Where's the elephant? Chant 2) Animal Actions Chant 3) What are you? Song 4) Elephant Rap	**Ee** elephant bed legs ten	**Pet care** food water a clean home love
1) What's the weather like? It's sunny. 2) Get in line, please./OK. 3) I want to see the space shuttle. Me, too.	Get in line. Buy a ticket. Go inside. Be quiet.	1) What's the weather like? Song 2) Museum Chant 3) I want to see the space shuttle. Song 4) Umbrella Rap	**Uu** umbrella bus jump run	**In the sky** the sun the moon stars planets a shooting star
1) I'm thirsty. Have a drink. Thank you. 2) Did you give it water? Oops. No, I didn't. 3) Who's hungry? Me!	Make a hole. Put in the seed. Cover up the seed. Give it water.	1) I'm thirsty. Song 2) Planting Chant 3) Who's hungry? Song 4) Apple Rap	**Aa** apple cat bat tag	**A plant's life** seeds water sun flowers fruit tomato
1) Feel this seaweed. It's slippery. 2) Let's put on sunscreen. OK. 3) I had a good time. Thank you. You're welcome.	Put on sunscreen. Run to the water. Splash in the waves. Dry off.	1) Feel this seaweed. Song 2) Seaside Chant 3) I had a good time. Song 4) Sounds Rap 3	Alphabet remainders: **Kk** **Ll** **Nn** **Qq** **Vv** **Ww** **Xx** **Yy** **Zz**	**In a tide pool** a shell a crab a rock a starfish seaweed

Extra songs   SuperTots Theme Song, Hello! Song, Clean-up Song, Goodbye Song, ABC Song

We would like to thank the following for their valuable input into this project as reviewers and piloting teachers:

Susan Brennan, Hyogo, Japan
Carol Harold, Maria Gerrard, Peter Karamishef, Kumamoto YMCA, Japan
Katherine MacKay, Osaka YMCA, Japan
Reiko Tada, GET: Group of English Teachers, Nishinomiya, Japan
Ban Guem Im, Kim Miyoung, Zoe Mason, Lee Young Jin, Park Eun Young, Seoul, Korea
Yin-Chun Cathy Chen, Kiddo Land, Taiwan

Also thank you to the teachers who have given feedback on the series at various stages of development: Chiaki Fukui, Michelle Philpot, Mamiko Tani, Petina Farrens, Yoko Sekigawa, Fumie Kojima, Julie Gienger.

My heartfelt thanks to all the young learners who were my 'guinea pigs' and helped me develop my ideas and philosophy. Thanks also to my teacher-students: Atsuko Kawamata, Yukiko Hirata, Yuko Igarashi, Eiko Sekine, and Yasuko Kobayashi, for their invaluable time and advice on this project.
Aleda Krause

My thanks to the many children, who, over the years provided the fun and inspiration in my teaching. Many thanks to Rie Tsuchiya and Hiromi Shirose who shared the classroom and magical moments with me. But most of all, my thanks to Justin, who, through everything, taught me how to laugh with all my heart.
Michelle Nagashima

Thank you to Lewis Chan, Chan Ming Sum, and Chan Ming Yan for their help with the craft pages, and to Mio Morikawa, Cara Nishiyama, Etsuro Nishiyama, and Lisa Nishiyama for their help with the pet care page.